The Wealthy Author

By
Marc Guberti

Your Free Gift

WEALTHY AUTHOR SUMMIT

As a way of thanking you for your purchase, I am offering you a free ticket to the Wealthy Author Summit.

The Wealthy Author Summit showcases an ever growing list of speakers who will teach you how to write, launch, and sell your books—and use your books to generate a full-time income.

If you are interested in making consistent passive income from your books, then I recommend getting your free ticket for the **Wealthy Author Summit** which contains the insights that will allow you to reach the next level.

wealthyauthorsummit.com

Table Of Contents

Introduction..1

Chapter 1: How Many Books Should You Publish..........3

Chapter 2: Planning Out Your Next Book.......................6

Chapter 3: Allocating Time To Write Your Book...................15

Chapter 4: Making Sacrifices...........................26

Chapter 5: The Marketing Channels................................35

Chapter 6: Winning With The Email List...........................43

Chapter 7: Leveraging Social Media For Boosted Book Sales....63

Chapter 8: Your Book Is The Beginning Of The Funnel.........76

Chapter 9: Turning Your Book Into Additional Products.........87

Conclusion..99

Introduction

Imagine your books making passive income that can support your lifestyle. It's possible and we all know it. Whether we see the author making thousands of dollars in passive income each month or the author making 7-figures from their books, we know it's possible.

So why then do very few authors know how to achieve wealth from their books?

By definition, achieving wealth from your books means getting them into the hands of many readers…so you also get to create a big impact through your work.

Part of the problem is that not everyone knows how their writing leads to wealth. It's one thing to grind and put in the work. It's another thing to focus your time into the right areas that result in more income.

I've met with hundreds of authors. Some of them are trying to get started and make enough sales so they can see self-publishing is something that can work. Other authors I got to meet were deep into the 6-figure range with some making 7-figures from their books each year.

The Wealthy Author has a different mindset from the rest. Combine that with the fact that these authors know what it takes to sell enough books to become wealthy, and it's no wonder some authors make full-time incomes from their books.

In the upcoming pages, you will learn the strategies of wealthy authors and how you too can join them with your books.

Let's get started.

Chapter 1
How Many Books Should You Publish?

Traditional publishers only allowed authors to publish a new book every 1-2 years. If you wrote too many books, the publishers would have a hard time marketing each of those books.

First, you'd actually have to get a publisher to accept your book. Many successful authors were denied by dozens of publishers before one finally said yes. When you got accepted, you'd then complete a new book every few years and the publisher would then "promote" your book (you'd still end up doing most of the work. This nugget applies to this day).

Self-publishing entered as the advent which allowed anyone to become an author. Authors previously rejected by publishers could now publish their titles and reach readers. Some authors who got rejected ended up self-publishing their books with great success.

Most of the talk about self-publishing is how revolutionary it was since anyone could now publish their own book.

But self-publishing also did something else. It gave us more options and models for writing and marketing our books.

While you'll still see some people only publish a book every few years and become successful on that model, there are more people who recommend writing as many books as you can.

I for one have written over 20 books while others have written 50 or even over 100 books. The idea behind publishing more books is that each book presents another opportunity for passive income. If you can make $100/mo from each book you publish, then it reasons that the more books you publish, the better.

That is why we begin this book with a question that has gained a lot of steam since the dawn of self-publishing: How many books should you publish if you want to become wealthy?

By the end of this book, you'll have your answer. The vague answer to this question is that you should publish as many books as you can write AND market. If you write a bunch of books but don't do any marketing, you won't become a wealthy author. It's better to publish 1 book that you market really well instead of publishing 10 books that you don't market very well.

But if you can publish 10 books and effectively market all 10 of them, that would be even better.

This question boils down to effective marketing. If you can achieve your definition of effective marketing for three books each year, then write three books each year.

The amount of books I write and publish each year depends on how many I believe I can comfortably produce and market. That number varies each quarter.

If you are just starting out, I recommend getting comfortable with publishing many books. Get comfortable with writing at least 1,000 words each day and publish new books in bulk. You learn new things about the writing and launching processes each time you publish a new book.

You can do all of the reading and watch all of the videos and courses you want about self-publishing, but you only truly learn when you publish your own book. That's why I encourage all starters to focus on publishing as many short books as possible. Each one gets you closer to your reliable passive income makers.

Chapter 2

Planning Out Your Next Book

How do you take this one idea and turn it into 50, 100, or over 200 pages of epic content? The answer is with a plan.

The truth about planning out your next book is that it's not nearly as complicated as it sounds. You can have a solid book plan within 30 minutes, and as you write more books, you might cut that time down to under 10 minutes.

Planning out your next book comprises of three steps:

1. Identify your book topic
2. Brain dump
3. Create a "Socratic Outline"

The first step is straightforward. Come up with a topic that will make up your next book. When you're deciding between topics, aim for a topic that you know well and can easily write about.

Notice how research isn't one of the steps here. I intentionally write books about stuff I'm already familiar with. I spent years reading through books about building a self-publishing brand, interviewed over 30 people for my Wealthy Author Summit event, and interviewed even more authors on the Breakthrough Success Podcast.

Some day, I want to write books on real estate. However, those book ideas are on the back burner. I have some background knowledge, but I'd have to do research so I fully know what I'm writing about.

While I could write the book before making my first deal, it would dramatically increase the quality of the book if I could make a deal first.

I bring this up because sometimes people feel like they need to do A, B, and C before they can write a book on X.

As long as you can provide meaningful value that helps the reader achieve the promise you make in your book, you can get started on that book.

So if you're a real estate whiz who knows much of the process but hasn't made a deal yet, write the book and see what happens. You won't be able to provide any firsthand experiences in your book, but the strategies and tactics you heard of may help your readers with their first deal. You can also interview people for your book and find examples of people crushing it in real estate.

There are several MLB managers who didn't play at the professional level including Jack McKeon whose 2003 Marlins team went on to win the World Series that year. He doesn't have a single day of experience playing as an MLB player and yet he led an MLB team to a World Series victory. If you didn't play professional baseball, you can still be a manager if you know enough about the sport.

That's because being a manager requires a different skill set from an MLB player. Writing about real estate requires a different skill set from actually investing in real estate.

If you didn't make your first real estate deal yet (or your equivalent), you can still be an author of a real estate book if you know enough about real estate. You'd actually learn a lot about real estate just by writing that book.

So you don't need to accomplish A, B, and C to write the book on X. If you know your stuff, you can write the book. I'd advise doing more research for a book like this to provide a valuable experience for your readers. However, since we don't want to do much research for our first book, it's best to save the real estate book (or your equivalent) for later.

When you know your stuff about the topic, it comes more naturally and less research is required. Remember, we want to choose a book topic we'd have to do very little research on. When you aren't writing your book or working on your business, you should be learning. That's the time when you do research on your book topic and other areas that fascinate you.

Once you identify your book topic, the next step is to conduct a brain dump. In a brain dump, you simply write down everything you know about that topic. Don't worry about organizing it. We'll cover that in the final step.

Just write a list of everything you know about the topic.

Once you complete that step, the final step is to create a Socratic Outline. Similar to a traditional outline, you organize the brain dump into the sections and chapters that will form your book.

However, the Socratic Outline takes the traditional outline one step further.

When you have your final list of topics, look at them from the reader's perspective. If your readers bought your book and only got access to your outline, what questions would they have.

Part 1 of this book focuses on writing your book. Putting myself in a typical reader's perspective, I asked myself these questions:

- How can I write the book faster?
- What are some productivity hacks the top writers are using?
- How does this lead to money?
- How long should my book be?
- How can I improve my writing?
- What if I get stuck?
- What topic should I write about first?

Some of those questions may resonate with you. You might also look at that list and see one of your questions is missing. You get better at covering more ground with each book by taking the time to understand your audience. We'll go deeper on understanding our audience soon enough.

For now, come up with as many questions you'd have as possible. Now your outline may look something like this:

Book Section #1
    Sub-Topic #1
        Question #1
        Question #2
        Question #3
    Sub-Topic #2
        Question #1
        Question #2
        Question #3

    (continue with as many subtopics as you need)

Book Section #2
(and then continuing on this pattern until the Socratic Outline is finished)

The great thing about the Socratic Outline is that it gives you more content to cover. Most authors get excited with their new book idea only to realize 5,000 words later that they can't continue with this book.

The first book I attempted to publish on Kindle never got finished. I stopped at 3,000 words. I realized I chose the wrong idea and couldn't continue with it. While I could easily pick myself up from that now, it was a major setback when I first started.

I then had to start writing another book wondering if I'd complete it. You have to tune out any of the internal voices that say you can't do it and replace them with positive thoughts (i.e. "I will finish this book and it will powerfully impact readers"). I finished writing that 2nd Attempt book and self-published it. If you've faced setbacks before in your self-publishing journey, believing in your ability to cross the finish line will help make this time different.

How The Socratic Outline Can Turn You Into A Wealthy Author
We are still on the writing portion of this book. We'll go deeper into launches and marketing later. However, it's important to discuss how books make money.

We all know the basic way books make money. Someone buys your book and you earn a royalty for each sale. If you price a Kindle book between $2.99 and $9.99 on KDP, you'll get a 70% royalty for each sale. Paperbacks and audiobooks are a bit more complicated but you'll earn a royalty from them either way.

But this isn't the only way you can make money as an author. In fact, few wealthy authors only make money from the book royalties.

If you only see book royalties as what fuels wealthy authors, you are missing an enormous part of the model.

After interviewing over 30 authors as part of the Wealthy Author Summit (it's evergreen so you can still watch the sessions at wealthyauthorsummit.com), I discovered that they don't rely on book royalties for their income.

Instead, they use the content within the book as an income generator.

We've already spent a good amount of time together, and we're going to spend more time together as you continue reading. You might have bought this book before knowing much about me. In that case, a relationship is building. On the other side of the coin, you might have known me very well before grabbing your copy. In this case, a relationship is getting nurtured.

When someone reads your book, a relationship is getting built or nurtured. And people buy from those who they know, like, and trust.

Not to discount book royalties as a source of income, but this is where a little extra cash each month from royalties turns into wealth…

If you have a coaching program, you need to mention that in your book. People who read your nonfiction book have already expressed an interest in learning from you. If you present that opportunity, some of your readers will contact you and ask for more info. Some of my clients first came to me because they read one of my books and learned that I coach clients.

So where does the Socratic Outline come in all of this?

During the outlining process, ask yourself some of the questions that can lead into your coaching or something else you offer. Earlier I mentioned the Wealthy Author Summit. It's something that fits all of the themes of this book. While I could mention it every page, this book would quickly turn into an all-out pitch for the summit which you wouldn't enjoy reading and I wouldn't enjoy writing.

Just because you're reading this book now doesn't mean you have to continue. And I respect the time you're committing towards the contents of this book.

So instead of turning this into an all-out pitch, I organically sprinkle the summit where it fits. In my book Content Marketing Secrets, I mention what I learned from interviews from the Content Marketing Success Summit (this summit is also evergreen over at contentmarketingsuccesssummit.com)

If you've helped people through your coaching, share one of the stories in your book. Mention something like, "my client [name of client]" to subtlety promote the fact that you're a coach who helps clients get great results.

If you lightly touch on a topic you covered more extensively in another book, let your readers know that you covered more ground on that topic in your other book.

If you don't have a product to your name but recommend a product, become an affiliate for that product and link to it in your book. While you can't include clickable links in paperbacks or audiobooks, you can include clickable links in a Kindle book.

If you have a book or training course, include in your outline when you'll talk about that product and HOW you'll talk about it.

This approach also works if you are a fiction author. You can write series and use each book to promote the rest of the series. You can become a public speaker on the key themes of your book and share you're a public speaker at the end of your book. You can even create a training course on writing a fiction book and mention that at the end.

Yes, for fiction authors, you have to be more creative. You can't just write a novel and say "Go check out my product," during the climax. However, it is just as possible for anyone to make money *inside* of their book as it is to make money from the royalties.

As you create your outline, think of how you will make money inside of your book and work those components into the outline.

Chapter 3

Allocating Time To Write Your Book

Planning your next book will make the writing process easier. The clarity will allow you to write your book faster. However, no outline allows you to escape the writing process itself.

You still need to allocate time in your day for your book. For professional writers, this is easier. They're writing away for most of their waking hours. For a side hustler, employee, full-time entrepreneur, or anyone else with many responsibilities, it's not as easy to find several hours to write new content each day.

However, you don't need to spend several hours writing your book each day. This is a big misconception. When most people think of writing a book, they think of this mammoth of a project that takes an intense amount of uninterrupted work. I think this misconception emerges as we hear stories of people who spent years writing a single book.

In the self-publishing game, you need to get your books out faster than that. You should write multiple books each year instead of spending multiple years writing one book.

So when it comes to allocating your time, you don't need to invest hours each day to writing your books. You can start with something as small as 30 minutes per day. If you type at the average rate of 40 words per minute, you would have typed 1,200 words for your book that day. As you continue to create more content, you'll type faster and ideas will flow more easily.

If you get that same 40 WPM up to 50 WPM, then you'll write 1,500 words during each 30 minute writing session. Squeeze in three of these writing sessions each day (one in the morning, one in the afternoon, and one in the evening), and you'll write 4,500 words for your book each day.

It's easy for anyone to find two 30 minute pockets in their day to focus on writing books. Look no further than the bookends of the day. Wake up 30 minutes earlier to write those 1,500 words and stay up 30 minutes later to finish up.

Some people may argue that the afternoon is more difficult…that their schedules are so busy and no one else would understand. If you watch TV, surf YouTube, get involved in gossip, browse Facebook, have a lunch break, talk with people who add no value to your life, or do something similar, you have more than enough time for a third writing session in the day.

We all make sacrifices without realizing it. We are either sacrificing the short-term for the long-term or the long-term for the short-term. The short-term pleasures feel good now, but if you're in the same spot five years later as you are now, that won't feel very good.

Look for as many 30 minute pockets as you can find. You don't need to commit several hours straight to your writing. You can get there someday if you make this your full-time career if that's the path you want to take. However, when you've got plenty of other work and family related responsibilities, you want to maximize your productivity. The more time you spend writing, the more your productivity is going to drop as you keep writing without stopping.

I recommend finding at least three 30 minute pockets instead of at least two 45 minute pockets because we can stay focused and on the task for 30 minutes. The Pomodoro technique suggests we go all out for 25 minutes and take a break for five minutes.

It's a great technique for a long writing session (i.e. a few hours), but if you don't have as much time to create new content, I recommend working the extra five minutes to reach 30. If you work longer than that without the Pomodoro technique, you're more susceptible to slowing down and getting distracted. Sure, you might write more words, but you'll write more words with three 30 minute blocks than two 45 minute blocks because you'll feel more refreshed for the new writing sessions. If you write fatigued, it will show in your writing.

Those are the reasons I recommend 30 minute intervals instead of 45 minute ones.

Hacks To Get You Into And Back Into The Flow
If you've read a few books or blog posts on writing a book, you may have come across this concept called the flow. The flow is this

concept where you keep writing, the ideas keep flowing, and it feels effortless to fill page after page with valuable content.

When you are in the flow, you want to write content for as long as possible. If you're at your 30 minute mark and have some extra time, keep writing if you're in the flow.

The flow is this state that every content creator wants to be in at any given moment. We only get into flow with built up momentum. You will almost never start a writing session in a state of flow. It's when you get your foot wet and write for a few minutes when you can possibly enter the state of flow…that magical place where everything else seems to fade in the background.

Just you and your computer.

While it's very rare to start a writing session in flow, there are a few hacks to get you back into your flow quickly so you best leverage each 30 minute writing session:

#1: Finish each writing session with an incomplete sentence: If you are in a state of flow, it's because the ideas are flowing easily. Sometimes it's best to hold back towards the end and keep some of those ideas in your mind.

The idea is that when you go to your next writing session, all of those thoughts resurface and allow you to re-enter the previous state of flow.

Naturally, the only problem with this approach is that we forget things. If you forget important details from your book, it can be frustrating. Even with an outline in place, it's possible to forget about new ideas you think of on the spot. I was guilty of this until I came up with a solution.

That solution is to wrap up your writing session with an incomplete sentence. Write the incomplete sentence in such a way where you'll immediately remember how to finish that sentence.

If you start your next writing session by finishing that incomplete sentence, the thoughts you had in your previous writing session will start to flood your mind. At this point, you may quickly end up in the flow.

#2: Follow the flow…not chronological order: The quickest way to get OUT of the flow is to put your mind in a box and restrict it's natural path. Sometimes you'll be writing a Chapter about Topic A, but your mind is firing on all cylinders with so many great ideas for Topic B which you're supposed to discuss in the following chapter.

If this is you, stop writing about Topic A and start writing about Topic B. Leave one chapter unfinished and start the chapter you're more excited to work on. When you're in a state of flow, follow the flow. Don't try to force your flow to conform to the chapter you're currently working on. When you read a story or watch a movie, you usually see events unfold in a chronological order. However, those events in the book or movie are not thought of or shot in chronological order.

Some authors know how the story begins and ends and they fill in the details as they go. If you are more passionate about a future scene than the scene you're currently writing, start writing about the scene you're more passionate about in that moment.

Don't take flow for granted. If it tells you to go somewhere, go to that somewhere.

#3: Work in a distraction free environment

The reason I recommend that you use the bookends as two of your writing sessions is because there are fewer distractions. You've got less interruptions at 5am and 10pm than you have in the middle of the day (even during that middle, I'm sure you can find a distraction free area for 30 minutes. If you believe you can, you'll start looking for alternatives and more opportunities to write your book).

You can be in the deepest state of flow imaginable, but if you get interrupted by some kind of distraction (i.e. phone call, music [only the distracting kind…some people like listening to music for higher productivity], email notification, etc.), it's harder to get back into the flow.

The 30 minute writing sessions are meant to be hard core. If you make them hard core, you'll write 1,500 words instead of 1,200 words. Keep writing and you may someday write 2,000 words in a 30 minute period. It's possible with enough practice.

If you find yourself getting distracted, move to another spot or remove the distraction from the environment if it's more under your control. If you get an urgent phone call, quickly jot down what you are thinking so when the phone call ends, you can refer back to your thoughts and re-enter the flow. I prefer to leave my phone in a different room when writing. Getting in the flow is hard enough already. Protect that flow in as many ways as you can.

Staying Energetic During The Writing Sessions
We've focused on 30 minute writing sessions and how many words you can hit during those sessions. However, even if you take all of the necessary measures we briefly discussed, not all of your 30 minute writing sessions will be equal. Some will be more productive than others.

Your energy level determines your level of productivity in each writing session. The more energetic you are, the better your writing sessions will be. This is why I have been recommending 30 minute writing sessions as your energy will dip as you spend more time writing content. If you want to write for an hour, I recommend taking a five minute break in between sessions as the Pomodoro technique suggests.

But regarding 30 minute sessions, there are ways to maintain our energy. We are at our peak when the day starts. This is when we have the most energy. Distractions and decisions haven't hit us yet.

To maintain your energy, you have to start with treating your body right.

Treating your body right starts with getting the right rest. While we should aim for at least 6 hours of sleep and ideally in the 7-8 hour threshold, you should consider napping daily. As you stay up longer, your willpower decreases. An effective nap in the middle of the day allows you to quickly reset your willpower and get back to high productivity.

Set a short 10-20 minute timer for your nap, get out of bed, and eat something healthy right away. I usually eat blueberries or a pear out of every nap because the food you eat matters just as much as the sleep you get.

If you eat a bunch of chocolate bars all day, your energy is going to crater faster. If you eat fruits, vegetables, consume protein, and eat other healthy foods, you will maintain your energy throughout the day.

Why Did We Just Talk About Food And Napping?
This is a book about becoming a wealthy author. You probably expected a bunch of ways to write more content and promote your books so they get more sales. While we tackle those two areas, you might wonder why food and napping made their way into this book.

Becoming a wealthy author isn't just knowing how to do it. I believe there are plenty of people who already know what to do. There are people who can recite what you need to do from A to Z, and after doing A to Z, you become a massive success.

But it's a matter of executing and making it happen. By the time you finish reading this book, you'll have the insights to become a wealthy author…if you take action. Eating healthy and taking naps allows you to rekindle your energy and take more action. The better you are at taking action, the more successful you will become. I wanted to emphasize this point before continuing onward. The strategies and tactics can take you to incredible places, but only with the proper focus.

Time, attention, and energy make success possible. You need all three.

Your Smartphone Is Your Secret Weapon
We all have more time than we realize. Using the bookends of the day allow you to tap into an extra hour of writing each day.

But you have one more tool up your sleeve…and it's in your pocket. Literally.

I'm talking about your smartphone.

We spend several hours on our smartphones each day without realizing it. While most people use their smartphones to scroll through different sites and respond to people, you can use your smartphone to write entire books without sitting at your desktop.

All you do is open up Pages if you use an iPhone, Microsoft Word for most other smartphones, and the Notes app if you have neither. Then, you start typing.

The winning formula for this is to find as many micro pockets of time throughout the day. If you take public transportation, you can write your next book on your smartphone during the commute. If you are waiting on line for something, you can write a few more sentences for your next book.

You use your smartphone throughout the day. Each time you turn on your smartphone is another opportunity for you to write another sentence or paragraph.

It may not sound like much, but let's put it into perspective. Let's say you write a 20,000 word nonfiction book. For every sentence in this topic that's above this one, we've got 14 sentences that cover 195 words.

That's an average of about 14 words per sentences. Now, some of the sentences are very short while others expand, but the average sentence for this part of the book is 14 words per sentence.

With this average, if you write 100 sentences each day on your smartphone, you'd get 1,400 words.

I'm not expecting you to keep track of the amount of sentences you write in your book. Most authors don't track that metric. However, it's encouraging for anyone who wants to become a wealthy author.

You could briefly stop what you're doing, write another sentence for your book, and continue anew with the other thing you were doing. You should take out your smartphone right now, write a sentence for your next book, and then return to this book. The content on this page will still be here when you get back.

And with that, you just got one sentence closer to finishing your book.

I understand that you won't go on your smartphone to write one sentence for a grand total of 100 times each day. However, you could very easily write 5-10 sentences in one go. If the average person can type 40 words per minute, it's just 1-2 minutes of your time to write 5-10 sentences. Since we're talking about a smaller writing sample size, you'll have an easier time coming up with the ideas and seeing that micro writing session to completion.

If you have a two minute space of time where you're on your smartphone, you could easily write an extra 100 words for your book. The technology we have presents us with so many opportunities it would be impossible to count them all. However, we have to be responsible with the devices and tech we have.

If two authors have a smartphone, the average author is scrolling through social media and consuming other people's content. The Wealthy Author is using the smartphone to write their next book.

Chapter 4

Making Sacrifices

We've talked about writing your book and finding the time to make it happen. Before we dive into the marketing, we've got one more topic to cover...making sacrifices.

You see, to become a Wealthy Author, you have to make sacrifices. You have to put in the extra time that average authors aren't willing to commit to their books. When they're watching Netflix, you're writing your book. You also have to be fine with marketing your books.

This is an important point because some authors prefer to create, create, create without doing any of the marketing. The end result is a bunch of books that don't get sales and an author wondering, "I put so much work into this but I'm not getting any results. Is the system broken, a sham, or too saturated?"

But the fascinating thing about sacrifice is that every action you'll ever take is a sacrifice. Reading this book is a sacrifice. You could be watching Netflix. Writing your book is also a sacrifice. You could, again, be watching Netflix.

But watching Netflix or any equivalent isn't a free ride. You're still making a sacrifice, but the sacrifice in this case is much bigger…

- You're not writing your next book
- You're unable to market the book you currently published
- Your dreams get pushed to the side

Every action you take is a sacrifice. You either sacrifice Netflix (the short-term) for becoming a Wealthy Author (the long-term) or you sacrifice becoming a Wealthy Author (the long-term) for Netflix (the short-term).

24/7/365 Isn't Possible
With this hard talk about sacrifice, you'd think I never take part in any of the short-term stuff. People often ask me if I ever take off from my work and enjoy life a little.

The truth to that answer is yes. 24/7/365 is this overhyped mantra that isn't sustainable. You can't be working all of the time.

I sometimes engage in the short-term stuff. While I don't watch Netflix, I do play pool. Other than that, I exercise (vital for success) and spend time with my family and friends. I play video games about once a month with other people, at their places and on their devices. If I'm going to play a video game, I'm going to play it with someone.

However, you don't have to succumb to breaks like these every day. The system that best works for me is to grind hard for five days and have two special days.

The first special day is "Side Passion Day." I take a different direction and pursue projects I normally don't pursue because I deem them as "Side Passions." I commit a day to these passions so they don't take my time on the other five days.

I also have an Off Day which is exactly what it sounds like. On an Off Day, I don't write a word for an upcoming book. I'm not on social media. I'm not scheduling the next email or replying to any emails. In fact, those are my digital detox days, so I'm not even on my smartphone that day. Honestly, the Off Days sometimes drag towards the end of the day because I run out of things to do, but they are worth it.

The first Off Day I took in a while was on Christmas Day in 2018. After remembering how much more positivity I had and how enhanced my productivity was, I made this a weekly ritual. It's been paying off ever since.

So if you have a Netflix account, don't delete it. Watch Netflix during the Off Day if that's what you prefer. All I ask is that you watch Netflix on your television instead of a smartphone of computer. Taking an Off Day means not using the same devices you use to work. During Off Days, strip your smartphone down to its flip phone capabilities if you have to use it at all.

Go outside. Spend time with the people who matter. Go somewhere interesting. Make your Off Days exciting.

If you have an entire Off Day to look forward to with a Side Passion Day as an added bonus, it's easier to grind on the other five days.

Becoming a Wealthy Author requires the continue balance between short-term and long-term sacrifices. Give yourself one day each week for short-term pleasures so they don't take you away from your work for the rest of the week.

Understanding Pareto's Principle Helps You Determine What To Sacrifice

Pareto's Principle is one of the most famous principles in business. Many wealthy authors live by it.

Reflecting on this, it seems as if Pareto's Principle makes it into most of my books…

In case this is your first time coming across this concept, here's what Pareto's Principle is:

80% of your results come from 20% of your work.

The concept is true, and if you look deep enough, you will discover what that 20% is for your business…the work that leads to most of your results.

Most people stop there. They acknowledge Pareto's Principle and acclaim that 20% of their work brings forth 80% of the results. This is the stuff you have to start delegating and sacrificing.

The people who stop at the acknowledgement only see one side of the coin. To every coin, there are two sides.

To Pareto's Principle, there are two statements.

The first statement is the one that we know well. 80% of our results come from 20% of our work. The second statement?

20% of our results come from 80% of our work.

That's a lot of work that only leads to one-fifth of your results. That particular small slice of work that you do leads to everything else.

The other side of the coin doesn't get much attention because it is the disgusting, greasy side of the coin. Most of the work you do leads to minimal results.

Can you still work with that in your mind? Most of the work leads to minimal results.

80/20 Done The Right Way
This isn't meant to discourage anyone. It is designed to change the way we work on the path to becoming wealthy authors.

The wealthy author understand this principle and look at both sides of the coin. They focus most of their time on the 20% of the work that leads to 80% of the results.

As for the 80% of the work that leads to only 20% of the results? That gets delegated or eliminated.

Why do something when you know it won't produce much results? The biggest mistake I see people make is they will look at every possible opportunity without honing in on one opportunity to maximize results.

If something doesn't produce much results, and you don't overwhelmingly enjoy that work, then stop.

If it's something that you still have to do but know it doesn't bring in the results you are looking for, then outsource that work.

Since 80% of your work produces 20% of your results, you should look to outsource 80% of your business.

Then you can focus all of your time on the 20% of your work that leads to 80% of your results.

Even if something seems vital for your business' survival, try to outsource it. Scheduling tweets is essential for my business since that's how I get most of my blog traffic.

Delegating that one task allows me to save hours of my time each week. Delegating my blog post pictures allows me to save even more time.

Opportunity Cost
For every minute you spend doing something, you can't spend that same minute doing anything else. That's the basic concept behind an opportunity cost.

If you procrastinate for one minute, you cannot be productive and get stuff done during that same minute.

If you find yourself not focusing on the 20% of your work that leads to 80% of your results, then you are missing out on opportunities.

I will provide you with an example involving money just to highlight the importance of looking at Pareto's Principle differently.

Let's say an entrepreneur works for five hours a day and makes an average of $100 per day.

With Pareto's Principle in play, one hour brings in $80 while the other four hours only result in an extra $20.

Let's say the four hours that bring in $20 get outsourced and the same entrepreneur works for five hours each day.

Now those five hours get directed towards the work that brings forth the best results.

Instead of making $100 per day, that same entrepreneur is making $400 per day ($80 x 5 = 400)

Sure, delegation costs comes into play, but it won't cost $300 per day at that rate.

Overall, a profit is made because the entrepreneur was able to focus more time on the work that brought forth the most results.

If you focus more of your time on what works, then don't be shocked if you get better results.

Expansion

You've figured out Pareto's Principle and focus most of your time on the work that yields most of your results.

But let's say you have multiple passions and want to start multiple businesses. Maybe you want to write books and create training courses.

You can suddenly find that extra time to pursue more adventures by delegating most of your work. Inevitably, you will temporarily disrupt your groove.

If you can focus all of your time on the work that leads to the most results, you will have to introduce more work that doesn't (in the beginning) bring in much results.

Then you discover what works in the new adventure you are taking and delegate everything else that doesn't yield as much results.

The quicker you master something and the better you master your time, the easier it will be for you to master anything else that you want to master.

Twitter was the first social network I mastered. I only mastered Twitter because I gave up on every other social network.

Now I am on several social networks and have thousands of followers on most of the platforms.

Master one thing and then expand from there. This is the key to becoming successful as a wealthy author. To make this a reality, you must not be afraid to sacrifice or delegate the activities that yield minimal results.

Chapter 5

The Marketing Channels

We've made it to the marketing portion of the book. We'll start by laying the foundation of what an effective strategy looks like and some of the marketing channels you should use to boost your book sales.

First, we start off with the strategy, and every effective strategy begins with a stated goal. Here are some marketing related goals to choose from:

1. Number of books you want to sell each month
2. How much revenue you want your author business to make each month
3. Number of pre-order sales you want for your upcoming book
4. Number of consistent monthly sales you want for an older title
5. Number of reviews you get for your books this month

The key for all of these goals is a set standard of measurement. Whether you want to measure all of these by month, quarter, or year, you need some way to measure them.

Setting goals is essential to becoming a wealthy author and correctly utilizing the various marketing channels you can use.

Now that you've set some goals, we can now analyze the marketing channels you have and how they relate to your goals.

For this chapter, we'll provide a brief analysis of each marketing channel with each marketing channel getting its individual chapter.

#1: Your Email List

Everyone seems to say that the money is in your email list, and for good reason.

While it's possible to become a wealthy author by not implementing every single marketing channel we'll cover, the email list is essential. And if something you do grows your email list, it's effectively growing your business.

But if you aren't actively communicating with your email list, then there's no point in building one. You should communicate with your email list multiple times each week at the very minimum.

People remember you when they see you more often. If you provide valuable content during each of those encounters, they'll also trust you.

#2: Social Media

I've consumed articles, books, videos, and training courses about self-publishing…and not all of them mention social media. This is where we begin to tap into marketing channels that can help if you know how to use them but aren't completely necessary for your path to being a wealthy author.

However, the reason some authors don't see social media as a necessary resource is because they take the wrong approach.

You don't make money on social media by promoting your books to your followers. I have over half a million social media followers and I don't make money by promoting my books there.

Instead, I make money by directing my social media followers to my email list through free offers and giveaways. Social media allows me to build the relationship and cultivate trust. That trust is very valuable.

The important thing to realize about social media and producing free content in general is that it takes time to see the reward. I've had people contact me saying that they've been following my work for years and finally decided to buy one of my books.

You build relationships first. Then those relationships result in sales. That's the social media game in a nutshell. The more people you can reach with your social media posts, the more relationships you get to build.

People like Gary Vee, Grant Cardone, and Lewis Howes build massive trust not because they crank out a bunch of products and ask you to buy them. Rather, they produce so much free content that it's hard to keep up with what they're posting in a given day.

#3: Blogging, Podcasting, And YouTubing

I'm putting blogging, podcasting, and YouTubing into the same category. They all have similar goals with different approaches.

The end result is that you provide your audience with free, valuable content. Within this free content, you invite your audience back to your site and promote a free offer to grow your email list.

While we get the idea of producing free content, it's not always something authors are open to. We take great joy in creating our work, but many authors prefer to spend more time writing books than producing free content.

Creating the content helps you build an audience while the books help you make sales. While you can use books to grow your audience (provide a free offer on the first page of your book that grows your email list. Wealthy authors do this so their free offer appears in the free preview Amazon provides for the Kindle book), having an audience behind you for initial momentum will make a big difference for your sales.

The great thing about creating free content is that it can make you money with the right mindset. In fact, what you'll read now will forever change the way you view producing free content.

Here's the cool thing about free content. With a very strategic and conscious approach can make two power moves. The first power move is to promote your book within your content.

One of my books, *Podcast Domination*, teaches people how they can launch, grow, and monetize their podcasts. I promote this book often on the Breakthrough Success Podcast because listeners may wonder what goes into launching a podcast and how they can profit from one. I also promote it in my blog posts about podcasting.

But the second power move is the one that no one except for a select few use. These few people are part of the elite. They're the role models, and this second power move can make all the difference between having a dominant brand and not having one.

Are you ready?

Create the free content with the intent of incorporating all of that free content into your books. That's the second power move. This is how some authors can write their books in a week or less. They've already written the book. All they do is organize the free content, add a few other tidbits, and buy a cover.

Now each piece of content you create can tie into a theme of one of the books you want to publish. You can list your book ideas and start producing free content around those topics. Let's use some of my past books as examples for how this would work:

Podcast Domination
Content Marketing Secrets
77 Powerful Methods To Get More Kindle eBook Sales
Outsourcing Domination
Pinterest Domination

With five book topics identified, I can get more intentional with the blog posts I write. If I write a blog post each week about a tactic you can use to get more Kindle eBook sales, I can turn all of those tactics into a book in a few months.

One YouTube video each week or solo podcast episode goes a long way in a year. Especially since many of us talk more than three times faster than we type. Get those transcribed and you've got the content for your next book.

This is actually surprisingly common. Gary Vaynerchuk's book *#AskGaryVee*, Tim Ferriss' book *Tools Of Titans*, and Seth Godin's *Whatcha Gonna Do With That Duck?* all fit in this category. The authors organize their free content, add a few things, and create masterpieces. Preachers create CDs and books based off their previous and free (for the most part) sermons.

But these books do well because the free content is organized… and we forget what we read. What's the last blog post you read? What was the last video you watched? Who created the last piece of content you consumed?

These are all questions most people don't know the answers to unless they just consumed some free content. Produce a lot of free content that provides value and allows you to build a community. Then, you can turn that free content into books.

Think of each topic in this book (i.e. "#3: Blogging, Podcasting, and YouTubing") as a separate topic that you can turn into a blog post. It's best to create deep outlines of a few books you're working on so the content ideas come more naturally and better fit into the book.

Tactics and strategies like these aren't as straightforward for fiction authors, but they can still work. My recommendation for fiction authors is to first publish the short stories and books you publish as blog posts, videos, and/or podcast episodes. That way, you provide your audience with a story and end up with a Kindle book at the same time.

We'll go more into how to use blogging, podcasting, and YouTubing from a marketing perspective in a separate chapter. For now, I wanted to mention them in this chapter and introduce those two power moves. Those two power moves alone can make a big difference in your career as an author.

#4: Amazon Itself
Amazon gives you many capabilities to market your books. They give you seven keywords to choose from and the power to boost your sales with Amazon Ads.

It's incredible how much Amazon will do to promote your books once you get momentum, but until you get that momentum, Amazon won't do much for you. You can either generate enough momentum with Amazon Ads or promoting the book to your audience.

Some authors generate enough of a momentum solely with the right keywords, but this is very rare. The keywords are essential for long-term sales, but you need to generate the initial momentum before the keywords (if you chose the right ones…more on this later) kick in and get those massive sales.

I am intentionally emphasizing that you need to generate the initial momentum because it's easy to hear a bunch of 6-figure author stories and think that you're set just by publishing an epic book with an epic cover. There's so much behind-the-scenes work and decisions that happen before a book reaches 6-figures.

Even for the authors who detail their systems in their books. It's still a lot of work that we don't see. Amazon will reward authors in proportion to how much work they put in towards providing value and optimizing their marketing until they get it right.

#5: People
We've got so many marketing channels to choose from. Each one we covered can literally put you in front of millions of people. But no matter how advanced our technology and marketing options become, the most important place for us to put our efforts is in our relationships.

To launch a bestselling book that generates passive income for a long time, it helps big-time to have a launch team behind your efforts. That means building relationships, getting reviews for your books, and encouraging people to share your book with their audiences.

Healthy relationships are essential for wealthy authors.

Now that we know the five key marketing channels, it's time to dive into each one. We'll start with growing and engaging your email list and then continue from there.

Chapter 6

Winning With The Email List

To win with your email list, you need to grow it and continue building engagement within the list. Doing one without doing the other leaves the money off the table. We've already went into detail about the email list, so we'll jump right into the tactics.

How To Engage Your Email List
We'll start with engaging your current list. This is essential because you may have some subscribers on your list you haven't reached out to in a while. This is also great practice as you're growing your email list.

If you get this part down, it's easier to communicate with the people you add to your list.

But you can't just email your list for the sake of emailing them. Each email needs to provide value and have a purpose. That way, your subscribers stick around and you get book sales. Here are some of the types of emails you can send out:

1. Anytime you come out with new content, email your list. While I let my subscribers know when I come out with new

blog posts and podcast episodes, I sometimes let them know about my latest Instagram picture (Note: I focus on motivating people and giving them the insights to take their businesses to the next level. My Instagram is @MarcGuberti).

2. If you find a fascinating piece of content that isn't yours, email your list about it if you don't have any of your own content ready to go. As a bonus, look for other people's content that comes with an affiliate program. You can make a lot of money just by promoting other people's products.

3. Whenever you come out with a product, let your community know. That way, you get immediate sales. In the case of Kindle books, these immediate sales can get Amazon's attention and result in more long-term sales.

4. Any industry news can make it into the next email.

5. Any personal updates or things about you. Don't do this too often, but mixing in some personal updates allows subscribers to know you better as a person. It's usually best to incorporate this within emails that lead up to one of your blog posts, videos, or podcast episodes. Don't make it too long, but insert whenever possible.

You have five primary reasons to email your list. You can easily turn that into multiple times per week even if you aren't creating any free content (which you should start since you read Chapter 5).

You can also engage your email list with autoresponders. Not only is this for new subscribers, but you can also offer your subscribers free gifts and then communicate with them differently if they take you up on the free gift.

I see some email marketers ask their subscribers to enter their name and email address again for another offer to put those people on different autoresponders. If the autoresponders are done properly, this will help with more sales and building the relationship on a deeper level.

Keeping The List Engaged AND Boosting Engagement
Even if you provide valuable content, it's not enough to keep your email list engaged. You're still competing with at least 100 emails each day that flood your subscribers' inboxes.

You can use these seven tactics to get more engagement from your email list.

#1: Weed Out People Who Don't Engage
Before we focus solely on getting more out of your email list, we must acknowledge another part of the equation. If you have 50,000 subscribers, and only 500 people open your emails, you have a problem.

You can get more opens, clicks, and sales with the upcoming methods, but understand that you should weed out unengaged people from your email list. Here's why…

For most services, having 50,000 subscribers on your account means spending hundreds of dollars every month. ConvertKit, the service I use, has a rate of $379 per month for 50,000 subscribers.

If you weed out the people who don't engage, you will save yourself thousands of dollars every year. To keep the email addresses in hopes of re-engaging with these people, you can create MailChimp accounts which allow you to have up to 2,000 subscribers without paying a penny.

With this important idea discussed, we can now focus on the tactics that will help you get more engagement from the engaged subscribers on your email list.

#2: Write Catchy Headlines
If you don't get many people to open your emails, it's time for you to examine your headlines. Mastering the art of catchy headlines is more important than mastering the email copy.

Eventually, you will need to master both, but if you write great email copy with a bad headline, you won't get many clicks.

On the reverse side, catchy headlines with bad email copy will result in more opens but less engagement after the email gets opened.

It's easier to fix things like clickthrough rate and sales once you get the open rate mastered.
So how do you write catchy headlines? Here are some ideas to get started:

1. Incorporate urgency
2. Build up curiosity
3. Personalize the email
4. Leverage trending topics, holidays, and other timely stuff
5. Use a buzzword or name a lot of people know

Understand that you have a limited number of characters to implement these ideas. If an email headline has more than 50 characters, then your subscribers won't see the entire headline.
If subscribers can't see the entire headline, they won't click. Short and concise is the way to go.

#3: Email Your Unopens
Each person's inbox isn't as crowded as a Twitter feed, but inboxes are crowded nevertheless. Some of your most loyal subscribers will miss your latest email just because there are so many emails in the inbox but so little time.

If these people get a reminder to open your email, some of them will take action.

You can create that effect by resending the same email to people who didn't open the email the first time (your unopens). I typically send out the second email 1-2 days after the first email gets sent.

All I do is change the subject line, and just like that my open rate goes up by 10%.

This is the easiest trick in the book as it takes less than a minute to reschedule an email that you already sent to your list (the only difference is the email's subject line).

#4: Consistently Send Emails

If you consistently send emails on the same days and at the same times, your audience will start to expect your emails at those dates and times. Some bloggers email on Wednesdays at 7 am, and their audiences know to check their inboxes for the message they received on Wednesdays at 7 am.

This is a common practice among bloggers. Depending on your audience, you can add fuel to the fire by increasing the frequency of your email. Instead of emailing your audience every week, try twice a week, and if you can, send daily emails.

Always stay in the frame of your audience's mind.

#5: Get Better At Copywriting

Now that we've explored boosting your open rate, it's time to get results beyond a higher open rate. Copywriting is an essential topic. I've provided a few tips you can use to instantly improve your copy.

- Use bold font and bullet points
- Focus on benefits, not features
- Always think of your customer avatar when writing your emails
- Ask questions
- Have a strong topic sentence
- Use a P.S. at the end of your emails because those get a ton of attention
- Subscribe to copywriting experts' email lists and pay attention to their copy. Not every copywriting expert brands

themselves as a copywriting expert, but they know what they're doing ;)

#6: Include The Link In Multiple Places

One of the most common emailing mistakes I see is when people send an email with the link in one location (usually towards the end of the copy). If you want to increase your clickthrough rate, you need to increase the presence of links in your email.

I typically utilize the same link 2-3 times in each email. Here are my favorite places to put a link:

The very beginning of the email. For some people the headline and first sentence are enough to get the click.

The middle of the email. This serves as a reminder. Your subscriber becomes familiar with the link, and with great copy just before that link, you'll get more clicks

The P.S. Some of your subscribers will skim through your email and quickly scroll to the bottom. Your link will be waiting, and with great copy, you'll get more clicks.

Some people place the link in as many as five places, but that number of link placements is usually reserved for lengthy emails or product pitches.

#7: See What's Already Worked

Look through all of your emails and see which ones got the most opens, clicks, and sales. All three of those statistics are votes from your community.

If you see a trend where your audience engages better with Topic A than Topic B, then give your audience more of Topic A and tone it down with Topic B. You may prefer Topic B over Topic A, but your job is to serve your audience.

With that said, if you despise Topic A with a burning passion, then stop providing that type of content to your audience. Some people may no longer stick around, but it's more important to do what you enjoy than find yourself stuck doing something you despise just for other people's approval.

The 4 Top Email List Building Strategies
Email list building is one of the most important areas of your brand. You'll get a dramatically more effective response when you send an email to 10,000 people than when you send a tweet (or any social media post) to 10,000 people.

There are plenty of ways to build an email list. While you don't want to master the wrong strategies, you also don't want to rely on one method.

For a very long time, I solely relied on Twitter to grow my email list. My efforts paid off as over 10,000 content creators joined my list, but I knew that to achieve monumental growth, I needed additional email list streams.

We understand the concept of having multiple income streams, but we also need to understand the concept of having multiple email list growth streams.

Here are the four best strategies to start growing your email list.

#1: Evergreen Your Social Media Promotion
Create posting cycles for your social networks and occasionally add in new content. Delegate posting and social media growth to an assistant once you know what you are doing. You put in the initial work to learn and can reap the rewards with very little involvement later.

In the long-term, all you should be doing on social media is engaging with your audience and posting messages that come to mind in the moment. Nothing more.

#2: Optimize Your Site For Maximum Conversions
If you get hundreds of thousands of visitors, but you have no method of converting them, then you won't grow your email list.

This email list building strategy focuses on the visitor's experience and getting them to subscribe.

As soon as visitors come on the blog, they are greeted by a welcome mat designed to get more opt-ins for a free offer. Pop-ups, the sidebar, and the blog posts themselves get even more opt-ins.

I use ThriveLeads to optimize my blog for generating more leads. It allows me to utilize all of the capabilities I just mentioned and more. AppSumo is another great option as well.

#3: Create An Affiliate Program
I am an affiliate for Michael Hyatt's Best Year Ever Course. Michael Hyatt has impacted a lot of people, including some of the

top players in various niches. When it came time to promote the course, many affiliates jumped on board.

The result?

In less than two weeks, all of the affiliates combined brought in tens of thousands of new opt-ins.

Many people would be happy if they got that many subscribers in one year.

Michael Hyatt was able to do it in one day.

I'm not saying that all affiliate programs lead to these types of results, but they can have a seismic impact on your business.

I grew my email list by over 25% by hosting the Content Marketing Success Summit and Productivity Virtual Summit. The first summit got me past 10,000 subscribers.

When you get a team of people to promote your offers, you can reach out to far more people than you could have ever reached out to on your own.

You can use a service like ThriveCart or ClickFunnels to create your own affiliate program. When you recruit affiliates, it's essential to communicate with them through a custom email list and a Facebook Group Page.

These two communication platforms will be more than enough to keep your affiliates on the same page for what to promote and when.

Michael Hyatt's course promotion was a launch which means there was a beginning date and an end date. In addition to running a launch style product launch, you can also run an evergreen promotion so affiliates can set their social media posts in a continuous cycle and constantly promote your landing pages.

#4: Use Facebook Ads
I recommend trying the other three before you give Facebook ads a try. The reason is that you don't know how well your landing page converts until it gets enough visibility. You don't want to use Facebook ads for a landing page that doesn't convert.

You also don't want to use Facebook ads for a landing page that converts well for getting opt-ins, but the autoresponder doesn't bring in any sales. Then you're losing money in the short-term even though you are growing your email list.

With that said, Facebook ads are the dominant player in the social media space. There are plenty of ways to optimize your Facebook ads, but I'll give you the basic math you need to run a successful Facebook ad.

You'll need to pick a Facebook ad that is measured by the cost per conversion. Before you run your Facebook ad, you should know how much a conversion is worth to you.

Let's say you have a landing page with an effective autoresponder. Based on your past results, you know that the average subscriber spends $5 in the autoresponder. If you can convert subscribers at $2 per conversion with the Facebook ad, you make a $3 profit for each new subscriber you get from the Facebook ad.

These are the ads that become successful. It's not just about optimizing your ad for Facebook standards, but it's also about optimizing your autoresponder so Facebook optimization is a worthwhile effort.

To take this strategy a step further, you can focus on promoting a webinar. Webinars tend to convert very well from opt-in and sales generation standpoints. When you have a webinar that converts really well, you can even make it evergreen so you don't have to continuously perform the same presentation.

These four email list building strategies will put your list growth in a solid position. Once you have the growth and engagement down, it's time to maximize your ROI.

10 Tactics To Boost Your Email Marketing ROI
Email marketing is the most lucrative platform for an online brand. It's so important that every other platform (i.e. your blog and social media accounts) should direct people back to your email list.

However, getting people on your email list is only half of the battle. The way you communicate with your subscribers determines their engagement and the revenue that you make. In this article, you will learn 10 tactics you can utilize to boost your email marketing ROI so your return is more worthwhile.

#1: Analyze & Learn From The Masters

In every niche, there is an email marketer who seems to have the entire process dialed in. Some of these people have written books and blog posts about the process. Others prefer to tell their audience through videos and podcast.

Consume as much of this content as you possibly can.

Content consumption is a great start for becoming better at email marketing.

Pay attention to the copy, how links are introduced, the frequency of emails, the subject lines, and anything else that interests you when you read their emails. Don't just settle for a few tactics. Pay attention to how the top email marketers in your niche implement these tactics when they communicate with their audiences.

You can also subscribe to top individuals' email lists who are outside of your niche. Even though these individuals are outside of your niche, there's still plenty to learn about writing emails that generate more engagement.

#2: Insert A Countdown For Time-Sensitive Offers

Nothing moves people like a deadline. For some of your emails, especially emails featuring special discounts, it will be appropriate to insert a countdown. Countdowns raise the sense of urgency.

It's no wonder that during a product launch, most of the sales come on the last day. The timer is ticking with less than a day left, and then most people take action.

This isn't something you can implement within every email you write, but when you want to make a point about an approaching deadline, use a countdown timer.

I prefer to use the MotionMailApp to make this possible. You may have your choice for a different timer, but this is the one I use and I commonly see used in other emails with countdown timers. You can get 20,000 free impressions every month.

#3: Email Your Unopens
Emailing your unopens is the single easiest and quickest way to boost your open and click rates. No matter how loyal people are to your brand, they will miss some of your emails. This is the nature of our busy world where email marketing is no secret.

Some people receive hundreds of emails every day, so it's normal for emails like ours to fall through the cracks.

To remedy this effect, you can create a second email and exclusively send it to the people who didn't open the first email. This second email is an identical. The only difference is the email subject line.

Since these people didn't read your email the first time, this swipe copy will be completely new to them. For many of my emails, re-sending the emails to my unopens doubles my open and click rates.

#4: Learn From Your Past Emails

Every month, I look back at the emails I wrote for that month. I look at their stats and determine which emails over performed and which emails underperformed.

Ideally, I want all of my emails to over perform, but some of my emails underperform based on my standards. I look at both of these emails and see what I did. Here are some questions to consider and answer as you learn from your past emails:

- What were the emails that came before this one?
- Did I clearly describe the CTA?
- Did I provide multiple opportunities for subscribers to click the link?
- Did I keep the email nice and short and just provide 1 opportunity to click?
- Did I use a P.S.?
- What is the flow of my copy?

Continuously looking back at your past emails will help you write better emails in the future.

#5: Include Bonuses

Including bonuses increases the likelihood of people taking action. While this is most commonly seen in product pitches where people say, "If you buy through my link, I'll throw in some bonuses."

However, you can incorporate bonuses beyond the product pitch.

You can offer a small bonus (i.e. 4 video series) to people who read your blog post and leave a comment. When Chandler Bolt started his podcast, he offered a free copy of his book (he even paid for shipping) to everyone who left a review for his podcast. With this promotion, Chandler was able to get hundreds of reviews and subscribers for his show.

While it would be very complicated to offer a bonus in every email you write, you can offer bonuses for the important actions you want your audience to take. And those important actions go beyond buying a product through your link.

#6: Write Great Copy
Copy is the make or break point of all emails. Effective copy will result in more sales and poor copy will result in no sales. As you write emails, you'll get a little better at writing great copy. However, the best way to write great copy is to learn from the copywriting masters.

For my copywriting education, I primarily focus on content from Ray Edwards. There are plenty of great copywriters on the planet, but Ray is the best to me. I've read his books and joined him in his product launches not just because I know his product is awesome, but also because I get to see his copy in action.

Analyzing email copy will help, but learning from a true master of the process will help even more. I recommend taking a deep dive into Ray's books and reading his copy.

#7: Benefits > Features

I don't care that your product has a bunch of modules, a constantly updating library of content, and swipe copy you can use for your funnel.

I care about a product that can triple my traffic, double my subscriber list, and give me a funnel sequence that will increase my revenue by 20%.

One product description focuses on the features. The other product description focuses on the benefits. People don't care about what you give them. They care about the benefits they will get from purchasing your product.

When you share a new piece of content to your email list, describe the benefits they'll get after they consume their content. What will they be able to do or have that they can't do or have now? Answer that question in all of the emails you write, and your ROI will increase.

#8: Send More Emails To Your List
No matter how great your email copy is, if you only send an email to your list every month, people on your list won't remember who you are. While some people recommend weekly emails, I recommend getting as close to daily emails as possible…until you're sending an email every day.

In 2017, I was inconsistent with publishing new content. This inconsistency in content creation led to an inconsistent emails unless I was promoting a product as an affiliate. Towards the end of 2017, I realized that this had to stop for me to have a successful 2018.

At the beginning of November, I decided to write one email every day that would go out to my list. This email would promote the blog post I had most recently wrote. Now I have emails written weeks in advance.

The best way to get more consistent with your emails is to write them before you need them. When I was inconsistent, I waited until the new content was published before I started writing the email copy. That's like hoping you'll always publish a new piece of content at the same time and day every week…even if you couldn't schedule anything in advance.

Sending more emails to your list simply means having the swipe copy ready well in advance. I write anywhere from 7-10 emails each week so I always have email swipe copy lined up in advance.

#9: Offer Multiple Pricing Structures
If you promote a product to your email list, one of the best ways to drive more sales is to offer multiple pricing structures. These pricing structures allow you to account for people at different stages of the journey and with different incomes.

For the Content Marketing Plaza, I didn't get many sales in the beginning because I only offered a $997 option. After some more consideration, I added a basic level and an advanced level to accommodate for people at different stages of the journey.

During my Cyber Monday promotion, I got many sales for the basic level and some sales for the advanced level. Neither of these levels were options when I first promoted the Plaza.

Getting a strong return for your email marketing efforts isn't just about optimizing your emails. It's also about optimizing your sales pages or promoting other people's well-optimized sales pages.

#10: Craft An Effective Funnel

Funnels are very effective for generating a strong ROI. You welcome your new subscribers with a series of automated emails designed to strengthen the relationship and promote one of your products or services towards the end.

The starting point of all effective funnels is an understanding of how you'll take your new subscribers from the welcome email to the last email in the autoresponder. You should always start off your autoresponder with an email that strengthens the relationship. A popular way to do this is including a picture of yourself in the email and describing the context of that image.

As you continue through the funnel with the product in mind, offer free content based on that product's topic. This will warm your new subscribers to your pitch which you'll make later in your funnel.

When you do make the pitch, include several emails that promote the product. No one email will get the job done. As you subscribe to more people's funnels, pay attention to how they lead you through the process. You can use that as inspiration for when you create your own funnel.

One funnel idea to explore is a Free + Shipping funnel for your book. The basic idea behind this funnel is that you offer your book for free and ask the reader to pay for the shipping. In most cases, this one transaction will result in a minimal net gain or loss.

However, the power of this type of funnel comes with the upsells. It's not uncommon for authors who use the Free + Shipping funnel to make hundreds of extra dollars from each opt-in.

Rather than tell you the model of an effective Free + Shipping Funnel, I'd rather give you the entire funnel for free. If you head over to marcguberti.com/bookfunnel, you can get my entire Free + Shipping Funnel for free.

Then, all that's left to do is plug in your information and start collecting leads.

Chapter 7

Leveraging Social Media For Boosted Sales

Social media is a powerful resource that allows you to connect with billions of people. However, it's also a place filled with trending topics and the latest stories. Social media is a double-edged sword that can either grow your business or drag you into a world of distractions.

The way you use social media determines what you get out of it.

For this chapter, I'll share some of the ways you can use social media to grow your business.

Universal Ways To Grow Your Social Media Audience
The more you learn about social networks, the more you'll realize they are all the same. The same basic principles and tactics get you the majority of the growth. Here are some of the universal tactics to grow your audience regardless of the social networks you focus on.

#1: Post Frequently

Each time you post new content, you get in front of your audience. Most people believe the word for this type of engagement is consistency. However, consistency isn't enough.

You can tweet once a month and still be consistent.

To win on any social network, you need to be consistent and frequent. After doing research on YouTube to see how YouTubers grow their audiences, one pattern emerged.

That pattern was more uploads. When the YouTubers shifted to uploading multiple videos each week (and some of them doing it daily), their audience bases grew.

Similarly, I saw a spike in blog traffic the moment I decided to tweet multiple times every hour. On Facebook, LinkedIn, Instagram, Pinterest, and every other social network you want to grow on, you have to post multiple times per day.

I know it's harder to do that on a video focused social network like YouTube. Upload videos once per week at the very minimum and gradually boost that number. And as a bonus tip, if you are uploading videos to YouTube, you might as well upload them to Vimeo as hundreds of millions of people view videos on that platform every month.

#2: Share Awesome Pictures

Social networks have increasingly become visual over the years. Some social networks like Instagram and Pinterest require pictures for you to post.

But on social networks like Twitter and Facebook, posts with pictures tend to get twice the engagement as posts without pictures.

The next time you tweet something or post on Facebook, think of what picture you could add to the post.

Now we're left with figuring out what pictures we should post. While we can dig through our cameras and post stuff from there, you can also create pictures on a tool like Canva. You can create pictures of quotes, artwork, and virtually anything else with Canva.

The key to creating great pictures is to see what is already winning. When I first tweeted quotes from previous Breakthrough Success episodes, I had a light blue background with white text. Some of those pictures performed well while others didn't.

Then, I started to see what other brands were doing. What did the most engaged pictures look like?

It turned out (for Instagram) that quote pictures with black backgrounds and a combination of white and yellow text performed the best. Quote pictures with white backgrounds with black text also outperformed the average quote picture.

So before you create another picture or use your camera again, look on the social network and see what works the best. You can use hashtags to find posts on the topic you're looking for.

As a bonus, scroll through the pictures and comment on each one. Commenting is an under appreciated way to grow on social media.

#3: Control The Traffic

Social networks are designed to keep users on their sites for as long as possible. With this in mind, social networks have no problem with showing less of your content and more of someone else's content if that other person gets more engagement than you.

Social networks also have no problem with changing their algorithms or even creating pay to play atmospheres. Social networks can make any change to the algorithm at any time.

Social media is a great way to get traffic, but you don't own any of that traffic. This is why many authors look elsewhere, but those who use social media and convert the followers into their own traffic give themselves an edge.

You convert followers into traffic you own by getting them on your email list. You do that by promoting your free offers and giving them to your followers in exchange for entering an email address.

#4: Share Other People's Content

You can only do so much on your own. To achieve continuous success, you need other people to help spread the word about your content. However, people aren't going to tell their audiences about your content just for the sake of it.

In my experience, one of the easiest ways to get others to share your content is to do something for them in return. I frequently share other people's content and let them know. Tag the person whose post you're sharing so they get notified that you tagged them.

These people will then notice that you shared their content.

Will everyone you tag decide to share your content? No.

However, you stay in their frame of mind. That's essential for getting shares and building relationships later on.

Set a goal to share other people's content at least three times per day. Whether you send out a tweet, post a picture on Instagram, or shoot a YouTube video, you need to continuously share other people's content so your content becomes more visible.

#5: Engage In Communities
Social networks at their core are designed to connect us on a deeper level. It is remarkable easy to find engaged individuals within your niche and then engage with them. The key is to find a community where your targeted audience gathers.

Twitter chats, Facebook groups, and Pinterest boards are some of the options you have. You don't need to find communities on every social network, but if you find some communities and participate in them often (by providing value, not pushing your content to them), other members in the community will notice your value and check out your content.

10 Social Media Tips For Authors
Social media is one of the most powerful avenues for traffic and connections. The only problem with social media is that it is also a

giant maze. Not everyone knows where they need to go, how to get the connections, how to grow an audience, and what they want to be known for.

Each time another person becomes successful or well-known because of social media, authors are seeing the importance of social media more and more. The truth is that every author only needs two things to become successful on social media:

1. Guidance
2. Dedication (the will to implement and make it happen)

Although all of the dedication comes from you, I will provide you with the guidance you need to have a smoother journey on social media. Here are the 10 social media tips that you can utilize to be more successful.

#1: Identify Who Your Target Audience Is And Focus On Them

One of the most important things you need to do before anything else is identify who your target audience is. There are many people who make identifying a target audience much harder than it needs to be. I am going to break it down into two questions:

1. What do you post about often (what is your niche and expertise)?
2. Who would find those posts valuable?

Answering these two questions will allow you to find your target audience. The main benefit of identifying your target audience is that you now know which types of people are going to engage with your content. Having an engaged audience is critical towards success on any social network.

Just because you have 100,000 followers does not mean you are going to be successful. The person with 50,000 targeted followers is doing better than the person with 100,000 non-targeted followers who rarely engage.

#2: Engage With Your Audience

Engagement is a two way street. You want to build an audience that engages with your content, but you also want to engage with your audience. Engaging with your audience allows you to see more than just a number.

Regardless of how many followers you have, it is important to individually know the followers who interact with you. I know a few people who comment on numerous blog posts (if you are one of them, you know who you are). I respond to all of these comments on my blog and respond to all of the people who share my content on my social networks.

Does this take up time? It definitely takes up about 30 minutes every day, but this interaction allows me to know my audience. Knowing your audience allows you to realize what type of content they like. In addition, some of the people I interact with ended up subscribing to my email list and buying some of my products.

Interaction allows you to get a friendship going, and friendship in itself is a two way street. That's why, "I owe you" is a common phrase. If one of your friends does something good for you, chances are you will do something good for that friend in return. Being friendly to your audience and engaging with them may entice them to do something in return such as subscribe to your blog or tell their friends about you.

#3: Post As Consistently And Frequently As Possible

Many people think that posting often is a bad thing because it will annoy followers. I decided to give it a try and found the complete opposite. Posting more consistently and frequently has allowed me to engage with my followers more than ever before, and it has also resulted in my blog getting a big spike in traffic that never seemed to go away.

For the tweeting in particular, I send out one new tweet every 15 minutes. Some people may think I would be annoying my followers at this frequency, but that is not the case. The truth about social networks is that many people are simply using social networks to check their activity for a short period of time.

The average Twitter user is never on the social network for more than 20 minutes at a time. That means most of the people who go on Twitter only see one of my tweets unless they log in again or scroll through my timeline. It is okay to post often, and it is also recommended.

#4: Use A Universal Avatar On All Of Your Social Networks
If you think of a business, you think of their logo. When you think of Apple, you see the white apple that someone took a bite out of. When you think of Twitter, you see the blue bird. Similarly to how

people think of the logo associated with the business, the people in your niche who think of you will think of your avatar.

Using a universal avatar for all of your social networks will make it easier for people to remember who you are. The easier it is for someone to remember you, the more often that person will consume your content.

#5: Do Not Be Afraid To Promote Yourself Often

There are many content creators who fear that promoting themselves too often will make their followers become unfollowers. This is a concept that many experts use to tell marketers to avoid over-promoting their products on social media.

However, it is okay to promote yourself. In fact, it is okay to promote yourself often, but only if you promote yourself the right way. The right way to promote yourself is by promoting your free content and opt-in pages on your social networks. It is entirely okay to tell people about the same piece of content twice (or well more than that) as long as the two social media posts are spaced out for a long period of time.

On Twitter, I go by a 4-7 day cycle depending on how my spreadsheets are organized, and I send out over 100 tweets every day. Someone would have to scroll down for a very long time to find any social media posts that repeat themselves.

As long as your content is valuable to your followers, they will not mind if you promote them often.

#6: Focus On One Social Network

More isn't always better. There are many social networks to choose from, and that's the problem. Many people create accounts on numerous social networks and have small audiences on all of them. It is better to have a large audience on one social network than it is to have a bunch of small audiences on a bunch of social networks.

When I started my social media journey, I decided to focus most of my time and energy on Twitter. It paid off nicely, and Twitter now brings in the bulk of my social media related traffic.

However, it is important to eventually have multiple social networks with big presences. The best way to approach this is by taking another social network seriously after you master one social network. After I mastered Twitter, I went over to Pinterest and continued to master the rest one by one.

The main takeaway: you need to eventually be on multiple social networks, but in order to have large audiences on all of them, take it one social network at a time and then expand.

#7: Identify Where You Want To Be Month By Month

If you want to do better on social media, give yourself monthly goals. Goals create a sense of direction and give you an idea of where you are heading.

What are some of the things you aspire to do on social media? Maybe you aspire to get 100,000 engaged followers, or you aspire to get more traffic to your content.

The aspiration is a starting point towards social media success. After you give yourself the aspiration, you need to identify the steps you are going to take to get there. It is important to give yourself steps that are neither too easy nor too difficult to achieve.

Gaining 100 followers every week is a great start. It's not far out there, but it's not incredibly easy either. If you are at that point already, raise the bar to 150 followers every week and keep on raising the bar as you accomplish the goal. Then, once you identify the aspiration and give yourself the steps you will need to get there, all you have to do at that point is implement.

#8: Be On Social Media Every Day

Just like everything else, social media requires practice. The more you show up and **do the right things**, the more likely you are to have the big audience. "Do the right things" is in bold because most people are already on social media every day. However, not all of that time is being used effectively.

Some people who use social media are using it to procrastinate. There are many videos and social media accounts to choose from. In essence, social media can either be your best friend or your worst enemy.

When I say be on social media every day, I mean you are utilizing it as an authors who interacts with likeminded people, not someone who procrastinates. Definitely use social media, but use it wisely.

#9: Do Not Let Social Media Consume Too Much Of Your Time

Social media is a great tool to grow your business and get more traffic. However, you need to have a good business and valuable content so all of the work you put in on social media is worth it. Just because you have 100,000 targeted followers does not mean you are going to make a full-time income.

Having that many followers does significantly help out in the process, but you need more than a big audience. You still need to find a good chunk of time in your day to create products and work on big projects for your business. That way, when you grow your social media audience, you can lead them to places that can bring in more revenue.

You should constantly be trying to perform the same activities on social media is a shorter amount of time. If you can do something in 15 minutes instead of 30 minutes, then make that change. I use Hootsuite to schedule hundreds of tweets per day in just five minutes instead of a few hours every day if I had to manually schedule them.

#10: Be Patient

Being patient is the most important tip on the entire list. Sure I went into more detail in the other tips about growing an audience and boosting numbers, but none of those changes happen overnight.

It took me 993 days to reach 100,000 Twitter followers, and most of that growth happened in the last year of that span. For more than half of that time, I had no idea what to do. I was struggling to grow my audience and was stuck at 1,667 followers for many months. Then, methods started to work, I modified them along the way, and now I have a large, engaged Twitter audience.

There is no such thing as an overnight success. All of the leaders in your niche got to where they are after years of work. By not giving in and learning new techniques along the way, you may become a social media influencer.

Chapter 8

Your Book Is The Beginning Of The Funnel

Understanding this truth is the key to making money with your book. It's easy to think that the relationship begins and ends with a book sale. This is one of the biggest mistakes you can make.

When someone buys your book, they put some of their skin in the game. Whether it's $2.99, $9.99, or some other price point, that customer put their hard earned money into one of your products.

It is this group of people that is more likely to conduct repeat business with you. Turning your book into the beginning of a funnel rather than the end goal turns struggling authors into wealthy authors.

When you hear about a 6-figure author, very few of those authors actually make all of that money from their books. It's the training courses and services they provide within the book that drive the sales and lead them to that 6-figure status. The few authors who make 6-figures just from book sales either make more money on the backend or are leaving a huge opportunity on the table.

Strategic Placement Throughout Your Book

While your book is the beginning of a funnel, it's not meant to be salesy. I occasionally mention the Wealthy Author Summit because it's a resource that I know the 30+ sessions in there can help turn you into a wealthy author. It's a resource I am eager to share because I know how powerful it is.

However, I don't promote my summit on every single page. I also don't mention clients, Breakthrough Success, the Content Marketing Plaza, or anything else I'm doing on every page.

Instead of doing that, I spread out the placements in a way that preserves the book's value. I'lll weave my offers into the conversation instead of making them stand out and forcing you to read a long pitch.

The next time you write a book, think of which offers you want to share. If you are a marketer writing a marketing book, mention one of your client success stories in one of the chapters. That success story will bring attention to the fact that you take on clients for your business.

You can also mention how one of your programs covers certain topics that you briefly cover in your book. This subtly brings attention to the fact that you have a program that you can link to in your book. While you can't use a hyperlink in a paperback book, you can include them in the eBook editions.

I have no goal on how often I have to promote an offer throughout my book. I just insert them into the conversation whenever they are relevant. If you think you'll sound salesy by including offers, you have to come to this understanding:

If you believe your offer has the ability to enhance the life of your readers, then not sharing those offers in your book is a selfish act that deprives your readers of that potential benefit.

If you know your offer can transform a life, you need to include that offer in your book. No way around it.

Promote Your Offers In The Bookends Of Your Book
While you should weave various offers throughout your book, it's important to use the bookends of your book to promote your offers as well.

There are two kinds of offers you need to promote during the bookends that go in different places. At the start of your book, promote a free offer that people can access in exchange for an email address. The goal behind this offer is to grow your email list since that's where the money is.

This is the only offer you promote at the start of your book. The more choices you give people, the more you will overwhelm them. You can promote one bundled offer where new email subscribers get access to all of the offers you're providing.

This free offer should be related to your book. I usually offer a free ticket to one of my evergreen virtual summit that is related to the book.

One smart free offer is a free copy of the audiobook edition of your book. Potential customers previewing your Kindle book will believe they're getting a steal and sign up for the free audiobook. The idea is that these people now have your book's content and won't buy the Kindle or paperback version.

So if you're essentially giving your book away from free but in a different format, why is this a smart move. Wouldn't this result in less sales?

Sure, some people may buy the audiobook version and not buy your Kindle book because they have the audiobook. Some people will buy the audiobook but also want the paperback or Kindle edition so they can more easily read along.

But even if a would-be buyer gets the free audiobook instead of buying your book, this is a smart move. To understand, we have to take a deeper dive. Let's say that you price your Kindle edition at the common $2.99. A 70% commission for your efforts results in $2.09 for your efforts minus a few cents depending on how long your book is. In the overwhelming majority of cases, you can expect at least $2 per sale.

So here's the question…

Would you pay $2 for a qualified lead? If your answer is yes, then you're starting to understand why it's smart to offer the free audiobook on the first page of your book. Even though people with the Free Preview option can see this offer and join your email list instead of buying your book, it's a $2 cost for the conversion.

Most marketers getting qualified leads at $2 per conversion from their Facebook ads would run those ads all day long. In the Facebook ad scenario, that initial money comes out of the ad spender's pocket.

However, when someone subscribes to your email list for the free audiobook, that isn't money out of your pocket. Some of the people who opt-in for your audiobook wouldn't have bought your Kindle or paperback edition. You can then use the funnel to promote the offers that you promote in your book anyway…and probably get more sales in the process.

Now that we've talked about the first page of your book, let's talk about the last few pages. It's during these last few pages where you can go deeper and use one of those pages to describe your offer.

Think of your book as a webinar. No one promotes their expensive offer at the start of the webinar. People would get turned off and leave. It's only after 30 or so minutes where the high priced offer is first introduced and then described in greater detail.

Your entire book is the extended version of those initial 30 or so minutes before the pitch. Your readers will like you more as they flip through more pages in your book. When people reach the end of your book, they have a deeper appreciation for you and your brand.

It's at this point where you can use 1-4 pages of your book to highlight some of the offers you have. Here are my recommendations for what to promote at the end of your book:

#1: Your other books. Readers like to read books, and your readers like to read your books. If you have written multiple books, mention those books at the end of each book you write. Some of your readers will binge purchase your books on the spot or the next time they are on Amazon.

For the eBook edition, make sure you have hyperlinks where your readers can easily go to buy your other books. If you mention your other books in each of your future books, you can create an infinite loop of your book recommendations that only ends when your readers have bought all of your books.

#2: Your recurring income offer. While I love creating products, it's common for us product creators to encounter a big problem: a lack of revenue consistency. Here's the picture…

You create a new product, launch it, and get a bunch of sales during the launch phase. Then, crickets. You need to create a new product and set up another launch schedule. In between product launches, your monthly income takes a big dip.

To avert this dip in income in between big product launches, I make sure some of my products follow the recurring income model. This is one of the reasons I offer products and services that bring in recurring income (usually masterminds for me).

While I like the nature of masterminds, you can also offer your coaching or something else as that recurring income offer.

#3: A Mid-Level Offer

Some of your readers will want to invest with you in a deeper level. While not all of them may have thousands of dollars to invest in a service, $47-$497 may not be out of the question.

I personally prefer to offer a product in the price range of $97 to $297. The reason I stay away from $47 is because that's the price of most of my All-Access Passes. If you join us in the Wealthy Author Summit, you'll have the opportunity to buy an All-Access Pass. Instead of promoting that offer, I would rather have readers sign up for the free version of the summit first.

To avoid making two $47 offers when I can easily raise the price and provide more value, I opt for a $97-$297 offer. That final price can go up depending on the offer I want to share, but $297 is the cap for mid-level offers in most of my books.

#4: Your Book-Related Service
Some of your readers will want to invest thousands of dollars into one of your services. This is the service you offer for those people…

If you have a service related to your book, promote that service at the end of your book. This should be a high-ticket offer that is meant to do most if not all of the work your readers would have to do.

Some of your readers will get a lot of value from your book but not know where to start. They may also not have enough time to do everything you suggest in your book. Your service can take the work off their shoulders and implement everything you taught them in your book.

If you do not have a service like this one yet, create one before you launch your book.

Provide Special Discounts For Your Readers
If you offer a special discount for your readers, you'll make your readers feel like VIPs. I tend to offer discounts in my books that aren't available anywhere else. Mentioning special discounts in my books results in more book sales which in turn results in a better Amazon ranking.

And the cool part about these special discounts is that you can track which sales came from which books. Anything someone buys one of my products with a coupon code that can only be found in one of my books, I know where that customer came from.

This makes it easier for you to track the conversion rate of all of your offers within your book. All you have to do is determine the number of book sales and how many people used the special discounts you provide in your book.

If I make 100 book sales and see that 10 people joined the Advanced Influencer Mastermind through an in-book discount code, I know that 10% of my readers are joining the Advanced Influencer Mastermind. It's ideal to use a special discount code for all of your offers so you can track each of them. You can use a custom Amazon affiliate link for your other books to track in-book sales of your other books.

If someone reading Book A decides to buy Book B through your custom Amazon affiliate link, you will see in your affiliate dashboard that you made another sale for that book. You can therefore tell that one of your readers from Book A bought Book B. If only five readers have bought Book A so far, 20% of your Book A readers are also buying Book B.

You can see in real time how many of your customers buy more of your products. And based on Pareto's Principle which we discussed earlier, 80% of your sales will come from 20% of your customer base. Knowing which products convert the most and bring in the most revenue can help you make adjustments when you include offers at the back of future books.

Fixing Leaks In Your Offers
Sure enough, we only get to see how much our offers resonate by offering them. In some cases, you'll hit a home run and your readers will take action on your offer. In other cases, you may offer something that isn't an ideal fit and fails to get traction.

But that's okay.

One of the great things about self-publishing your book is that you can always go back and edit your book. I can edit this book at anytime to add or remove content and offers. If I create another offer relevant to this book, I have the ability include that offer in future copies of *The Wealthy Author*.

People who bought the Kindle edition will have the option to update. The only people who won't get the update are the people who bought the paperback. For audiobooks, the same rule applies if your audiobook is on Audible. If you decide to offer the audiobook version as a free gift, you can change the email sequence to cover the new offer or eliminate the offer that isn't resonating with your audience.

In some cases, you may like the offer itself but want to test out a new sales page with a different link. You can prepare for this by creating a custom link that you can change when appropriate. For instance, I use the Pretty Link WordPress plugin to turn a messy link like sendmeto.teachable.com/gBSlQ into contentmarketingplaza.com/teachable.

If Teachable comes out with a better sales page than the one I currently direct people, I can go into the Pretty Link WordPress plugin and change where contentmarketingplaza.com/teachable leads my readers. That way, people who bought the paperback copy before I could make changes still get led to the right page.

You can do something similar with bit.ly by creating a custom link. When you need to change where that custom link takes people, do the following:

1. Change the original custom link into something else
2. Immediately turn the desired link into a bit link and give it the same ending as the original.

That's a little hard to follow without a video, so I'll provide a brief example using the teachable model from before.

Just for the fun of it, I turned bit.ly/breakthroughsuccesspodcast into a link leading to the Breakthrough Success Podcast on iTunes.

Let's say that I later decide this was a big mistake and that I want this same link to lead to Breakthrough Success on Spotify.

bit.ly/breakthroughsuccesspodcast is already taken, so what do I do.

I go into bit.ly/breakthroughsuccesspodcast and add a 1 at the very end to make it this:

bit.ly/breakthroughsuccesspodcast1

I then immediately turn the Spotify link into a bit.ly link and make it bit.ly/breakthroughsuccesspodcast since that link is now available again.

While the Pretty Link plugin method is exclusively for WordPress bloggers, the Bit.ly approach is accessible to anyone free of charge. When you create that custom link, I suggest only using it in your book. That way, when that link gets a click, you know it came from one of your readers instead of from somewhere on the web.

While this goes beyond the scope of this book, I also suggest conducting A/B Split Testing for any sales pages. If you want to learn more about A/B Split Testing, I strongly recommend Russell Brunson's 108 Proven Split Test Winners. If anyone knows how split testing works, it would be that guy (he runs ClickFunnels where a gazillion pages have been created and tweaked to achieve higher conversion rates).

You can get your free copy of Russell's book at marcguberti.com/108split

Chapter 9

Turn Your Book Into Additional Products

Earlier we talked about how your book is the beginning of a funnel. You can then promote offers within your book and get people on your email list.

But what offers should you be promoting?

Relevant offers of course. While becoming a wealthy author and achieving personal development are somewhat connected, it's not a perfect connection. That's why I instead choose to tell you about the <u>Wealthy Author Summit</u> which is related to this book.

In this case, the virtual summit was inspiration for the book. However, I can easily flip that model and use one of my book as inspiration for a future virtual summit.

While a virtual summit is an ambitious path that I don't recommend as a starting point due to the sheer work involved, there are other ways to turn your book into additional products.

One of the easiest and most common ways to turn your book into an additional product is to turn it into a training course. It's not uncommon for content creators to publish a $9.99 book and create a $997 training course which is 80-100% based on the book.

Due to preexisting perceptions and buying patterns, we can better understand buying a $997 training course than a $997 book…even if the book and training course contain the same exact material.

Take each chapter of your book, shoot a few videos, and turn it into a training course. I like to charge anywhere from $97 to $297 for those types of courses and include extra value beyond the book.

You can also turn your book into a mastermind, membership site, or a service. We will explore all of those options momentarily but kick things off with the training course.

Publishing Your Training Course
Turning your book into a training course is easy. You take each chapter of your book and turn it into a section. Over time, you can add some extras in the training course that aren't available in your book.

When you have completed the training course, you have a few options for how you can publish that training course:

#1: Teachable—Out of all of the options, Teachable is by far the best and the easiest one to use. While some options restrict your control over the course and monetization and other options are difficult to implement, Teachable finds itself in the middle.

I currently put all of my mid to high-end training courses on Teachable. They handle all of the technology and give you the ability to collect monthly revenue from your customers. For instance, I use Teachable to process the payments and provide members with the content they deserve.

Just as a special offer, <u>if you join Teachable through my link</u> (<u>contentmarketingplaza.com/teachable</u>), I will throw my Virtual Summit Blueprint training course for free (the course has a $97 retail value).

But Teachable isn't the only game in town. Here are some of your other options…

#2: Create It Yourself—This option is only for people who know what they're doing from a technology standpoint. If you can create webpages, order pages, email sequences, and have them all communicate with each other, you can go this path.

In my experience, this takes the most amount of time, and while it can be the most rewarding when you have it set up, it can get complicated even if you know the technology behind it.

When I create a course on my own platform, here are the tools I use:

1. OptimizePress and/or ClickFunnels for creating the webpages and membership portal depending on the current set-up
2. ThriveCart for processing orders and deciding between one-time payments or recurring payments

3. ConvertKit for creating the email sequences

Those are the tools you need if you want to do it all yourself. I don't recommend this path for your first course especially since you're already busy writing your books, but it is one you can consider.

#3: Udemy—The last two options on the list are well-known but require you to sacrifice some control over the way your training course is marketed and makes money. The great thing about Udemy and the final option we'll discuss is that they both come with marketplaces.

In other words, students on their platform can discover your courses through built-in search engines. On the other hand, you'll only attract students to a Teachable course or one on your own platform by promoting it yourself and getting others to join you as affiliates.

And Udemy is easy for anyone to use. Just like Teachable, it is a plug and play where technology isn't a problem.

However, Udemy is widely known as the site where every course gets massively discounted for as many reasons as Udemy can think of. You can price your course at $199.99 and rest assured that no one will ever buy your course at that price regardless of how good it is.

Udemy students are conditioned to wait for when Udemy runs a sale that can see your training course drop to as low as $10 and almost never higher than $20 during a discount sale. This helps your course get more sales, but it annoys me when I see my $199.99 course only selling for $15 at the very most.

This is why I no longer release in-depth training courses on Udemy. I still publish on Udemy, but that is for a repurposing strategy (some of those videos end up on YouTube and in my Teachable courses. It's the only reason I still create new Udemy courses).

#4: SkillShare—The last option for your training courses we'll talk about is SkillShare. While this part won't affect most people, you are only allowed to publish one new course each week. If you like creating a bunch of training courses each week, this isn't the right course for you.

Instead of setting a price for your course, SkillShare pays you for every minute your students watch videos within your course. SkillShare is the training course version of Netflix. For a small monthly fee, students get access to thousands of training courses. That's why you can't set a price for your SkillShare courses.

This model has pros and cons for training course creators. Students will be more eager to learn and fully take advantage of their SkillShare membership. As long as you promote your courses to drive the initial momentum, students should have no problem finding your course and consuming hours of your videos.

However, there are some important disadvantages to SkillShare. The first disadvantage is that people who create shorter courses don't stand to earn as much revenue from SkillShare. An epic 1 hour course doesn't have as much earning potential as a decent 5 hour course. If you create longer courses, this disadvantage becomes your advantage.

But the biggest disadvantage with SkillShare is that a longer course can go for more money somewhere else. In most niches, a quality two hour course can go for at least $97. If someone buys that $97 training course through Teachable, you make all of that $97 or $92.15 depending on your Teachable account (in the first level of Teachable, you get 95% of the revenue from each sale, but you can get 100% of the revenue from each sale by upgrading your Teachable account to a higher level).

To make $97 on SkillShare, you need your students to consume a combined total of 1,940 minutes of your courses since SkillShare awards you with $0.05 per minute watched on average. This is a much higher rate than YouTube and most of the similar options, but it doesn't make as much sense to put all of your training courses on SkillShare.

In this scenario, you have two choices to make $97:

1. Sell ONE $97 course on Teachable
2. Your students need to watch a combined total of 1,940 minutes in your courses (over 32 hours of content. This is the equivalent of 16 SkillShare students consuming every second of your course)

I'd rather sell one of something than hope that 16 of the students from SkillShare watch the entire course from start to finish.

Wrapping Up Training Courses

If you are creating your first training course, I'd recommend using Teachable. It's the easiest one to set up and provides the most revenue potential without investing thousands of dollars into the right software to do it all yourself (and knowing what technology you have to use).

With that said, I still publish valuable courses through all four of these mediums. However, I put the more in-depth courses on Teachable and my own websites because I have more control over the pricing, communication with students, upsells, and order bumps.

I hope this analysis made training course creation seem a little easier. It's no secret that I am encouraging you to join Teachable, even if you don't do it with my link. However, if you do happen to join Teachable through my link (contentmarketingplaza.com/teachable), I'll throw in the Virtual Summit Blueprint as a free gift to you (I charge $97 for this course for everyone else).

Turn Your Book Into A Service
Have you ever read a book that contained so many valuable insights and strategies that you didn't know where to start?

Have you ever read a book where you wish you achieved results just like the author or one of the featured case studies?

If so, you probably weren't alone, and some of those readers would have paid top dollar for a service to do the work for them.

Your book can take on many purposes, and one of those purposes can be to outline what you can provide with your services.

You should provide as much value in your books as you can so people end up asking you, "Your book is awesome but doing this stuff will take too much time. Can you do it for me?"

The next time you write a book, think of what the service would look like. Would it involve turning a book into a bestseller or taking an existing book and turning it into a stream of passive income? The service you can offer would be different depending on the book you write.

The great thing about offering a service at the end of your book is that you don't have to think about it or fulfill it until someone asks about your services. It's in that moment when you need to get the entire process in place.

Too many people spend all of the time making sure every part of their service is perfect that they forget about client acquisition. The moment you get your first client is the moment you polish the backend of your service to provide your clients with an incredible experience.

If you don't want to create a new service for each book, you can theme your books around topics that match up with your existing services. If you offer a social media done for you service and write books on different social networks, you can occasionally mention your done for you service throughout the book and have an entire page about it at the very end.

Remember, wealthy authors don't just make $2 per book sale. They set themselves up so they can make hundreds or even thousands of dollars from readers who are willing to invest deeper into their success.

Offering a high-end service can easily set you up to make thousands of dollars from some book sales. I've seen some services deep into the five and even six figures per year. If you offer a service that you charge $25,000 for, then you only need 4 readers to commit to that service to make 6-figures. If you get over 1,000 readers and present the offer very well, it is possible for you to make 6-figures from that audience.

Incorporating MRR Into Your Book
One of the big disadvantages of books and most products in general is that you have to keep selling them every month to continue earning what you earned the previous month.

If you launch a book and it goes on to make $1,000 that month, you need to make the same amount of sales the following month to reach the same goal (assuming everything else stays the same).

And most books don't go on to make consistent sales each month. It isn't long before most books lose their presence on Amazon to get replaced by the next well-marketed book.

In my own KDP dashboard, I can see some books that brought in a bunch of sales each month during initial release now struggling to make the same amount of sales each month. In this case, there are two solutions:

1. Market your old books again (Amazon Ads or a discount. We have a great session in the Wealthy Author Summit about Amazon Ads)
2. Write new books and leave the old ones behind (the common path for most self-published authors)

Eventually, in most cases, the book you publish today that is doing well won't be doing as well years later. While marketing can change that, it's something you should anticipate.

We talked about incorporating products and services, but there's one more thing you need to incorporate.

Enter MRR which stands for monthly recurring revenue. This is the road to wealth. Making millions of dollars from a single launch isn't wealth. It's getting rich for sure, but wealth is the ability for you to consistently and passively make more money every month than you have to spend on all of your expenses.

It's no secret that Amazon currently doesn't have a program set up where you can claim monthly royalties from all of your readers. The only way to get $2 per month from each person through book sales is to publish a new book each month.

It's the pages in your book that earn you the top dollar. So while you are promoting your products and services, look for additional options that allow you to generate recurring, predictable revenue.

That's why I frequently promote my Advanced Influencer Mastermind and ClickFunnels. In the Advanced Influencer Mastermind, I offer every session from every virtual summit I've ever conducted (we're now in the 100s for sessions), the Live Growth Experiment, and a new training course each month. Members in the mastermind, who I like to call AIMers, make a monthly investment to continue receiving my top stuff.

ClickFunnels on the other hand is an essential software that allows business owners to seamlessly create their own funnels. ClickFunnels has a starting price at $97/mo and affiliates receive a monthly recurring 40% commission on all members they refer.

I could promote one or the other, and while I'd like everyone to become an AIMer, I understand ClickFunnels make more sense for other people. There are a few people who decide to do both as well.

If a reader becomes an AIMer and joins the lowest priced ClickFunnels version, I earn a consistent $135.80/mo in passive income. If that person stays in the mastermind and ClickFunnels for 5, 10, or even more years, I'm still making $135.80/mo well after this book was published…just from that one reader

Now imagine if 10 readers followed this path. That would be an extra $1358/mo. Do you see how these numbers add up and build a foundation over time.Imagine making an extra $2,000-$5,000 each month just from a book that you wrote a few years ago…and that's not factoring in if your book continues to make sales and attract more people to your offers

If the Advanced Influencer Mastermind and ClickFunnels are great fits for your niche, I can set you up as an affiliate for both. Just send me an email marc@marcguberti.com and I'll get you set up.

If not, then you have to find another product, service, or software that allows you to generate monthly recurring revenue. The recurring revenue will put you on a path towards financial predictability which is essential for becoming a wealthy author.

There are a variety of offers you can provide for your readers. The key is choosing the offers that make the most sense, provide the most value, and generate the revenue you need to grow your business. Very few 6-figure authors make 6-figures from their books in the volume of book sales. This chapter alone is how most of them end up getting wealthy. The prior chapters were about setting the foundation so you could attract readers to your book.

Conclusion

The path to becoming a wealthy author is different from the path people see on the surface level. Most people see this path as a massive push to drive more book sales. While this is certainly part of the equation, it is the words in your book that make wealthy authors far more money than they could have ever made from book sales.

But regardless of how many books you sell, publishing your first book will suddenly give you leverage. It will help you get on more stages and land more clients…especially if you promote your services at the end of your book.

Writing a book is by far the easiest way to become an established authority in your niche. All that is left is for you to begin writing your first book or working on your next one.

The great thing about self-publishing is that you can always return to your published books and make updates. If you forgot to mention one of your offers in a prior book, you can change that so future copies have that offer included.

Your first book and every book after that don't have to be perfect. They just have to be complete. In the end, people won't remember if your book was the best written book they've ever read. Instead, they'll remember how your book made them feel and what kind of value they got from it.

This book gave you the roadmap for becoming a wealthy author. Now you have to implement. You will learn new lessons each time you publish another book that no other book can teach you as well. Books like these can help you avoid mistakes and give you a jumpstart, but experience is the best teacher.

Whether you find some time each day to write and promote your books or you pick 2-3 days each week to get started, you need to commit time towards becoming a wealthy author. And if you track it enough, you'll eventually come up on top and be the next wealthy author.

About The Author

Marc Guberti is a USA Today and WSJ bestselling author with over 100,000 students in over 180 countries enrolled in his online courses. He is the host of the Breakthrough Success Podcast where listeners learn how to achieve their breakthroughs. He coaches content creators on how they can attract more traffic to their content and boost revenue.

Marc's Other Books

Are you looking for your next book? If so, Marc has written over 20 books which can all be found on Amazon. Here's some of what is waiting for you if you search "Marc Guberti" on Amazon…

Content Marketing Secrets

Discover the key secrets for getting massive traffic and revenue

"This book is a getting-it-done guide for going big in small, manageable steps. Marc has put the playbook together for you." --**Andy Crestodina, author of Content Chemistry**

Podcast Domination

Discover the ultimate podcasting strategies that will help you launch, grow, and monetize your show

"Thorough coverage of the subject. Many books in the topic seem to be teasers to sell premium content. This book is not like that - he covers all topics." — **Amazon Review**

77 Powerful Methods To Get More Kindle eBook Sales

This book provides effective methods that, when utilized, will allow you to see a boost in your Kindle eBook sales.

"For what I paid, I got a LOT of knowledge!! It's worth more in my view. Would have gladly paid double." — **Amazon Review**

Get Your Free + Shipping Book Funnel

A funnel is critical for your business' success. But not all funnels are created equal. This funnel is the same one that bestselling authors use to make 6-figures on the backend of their book sales.

Here's what you get with the Free + Shipping Book Funnel:

- An opt-in page for collecting email addresses and telling people about your awesome book
- A thank you sales page where you can promote an upsell
- An order confirmation page
- The ability to edit the funnel so you can add more upsells later on

If you want your free funnel so you can start a Free + Shipping promotion for your book, be sure to grab your free funnel here: marcguberti.com/bookfunnel

Join Us In The Mastermind

Do you want to become an influencer in your niche who makes money from all of that work you're doing?

If you are someone who feels like there's a disconnect between how much time you put in and how much money you're actually making, the Advanced Influencer Mastermind is probably for you.

As an AIMer (a member of the mastermind), here's what you'll receive:

- 1 new training course from me each month that I'll charge anywhere from $97 to $997 for to non-AIMers
- All past training courses that I have offered to AIMers
- Every session from every virtual summit I ever do ($1000s of dollars in value)
- Live Growth Experiment Series: discover what I am doing in real time to grow my business
- Plus some other goodies :)

If you join the Advanced Influencer Mastermind and use the coupon code "WEALTHYAUTHORBOOK," I'll reduce the price to $7 for the first month of your membership just so you can get a feel for how the mastermind works.

You can learn more about the mastermind at contentmarketingplaza.com/mastermind

Done For You Business Book Writing + Marketing

Do you want to be an author of a successful book but don't have the time to make it happen?

I understand that feeling. You want to write a book but business and everything else seems to get in the way.

If you resonate with the previous statement, you may want to consider having me write your business book for you and assisting you in the marketing and monetization.

I can only take on a select number of clients and book topics at a time. If you are interested in this done for you service, please schedule a strategy call with me by heading over to marcguberti.com/strategy.

I hope to hear from you and see how I can help you grow your author business and achieve your breakthrough.

www.ingramcontent.com/pod-product-compliance
Lightning Source LLC
Chambersburg PA
CBHW020544220526
45463CB00006B/2182